MAY GO)

IN YOUR RACE OF LIFE

HOPE YOU ENJOY

BLESSINGS

Mark Bidell

About the Author

Malcolm Rothwell is a retired Methodist minister and a marriage counsellor. He was greatly influenced by a 30 day silent retreat; a conversion experience that saved his spiritual bacon. He leads retreats and has a ministry of spiritual accompaniment. He is a former Chair of the Retreat Association and the Methodist Retreat and Spirituality Network. He has written two books; *Journeying with God*, and *Sense and Nonsense*, conversations with a clown about spiritual things.

This book is dedicated to my lovely wife Lucy

Malcolm Rothwell

RUNNING THE RACE - FINDING GOD IN THE LONDON MARATHON

AUSTIN MACAULEY
PUBLISHERS LTD.

A CIP catalogue record for this title is available from the British Library.

ISBN 9781785542787 (Paperback)
ISBN 9781785542794 (E-Book)

www.austinmacauley.com

First Published (2016)
Austin Macauley Publishers Ltd.
25 Canada Square
Canary Wharf
London
E14 5LQ

Acknowledgments

I am really grateful to Jacqui Lea of the Hopeweavers community who first put the idea of writing a book into my head. She also read the first draft and gave me lots of ideas and found many mistakes. She also gave me two interesting books about the Olympic athletes Harold Abrahams and Eric Liddell. Their fame has been recorded in the film *Chariots of Fire*. Many thanks also to Audrey Hollingbery who read the first draft and made lots of corrections. I am also grateful to Richard Hollingbery who, among other things, gently let me know that Petersfield is in Hampshire and not in Surrey! I am eternally thankful to my wife, Lucy, for her love, constant support and patience, not to mention her great skill at massaging my aching legs. I really appreciate all my family, friends and Christian brothers and sisters who have supported me with their prayers and generous financial gifts for Help the Hospices. Last, but by no means least, many, many thanks to family and friends who turned up on the Big Day to cheer.

Contents

Introduction

Running

Although this book is about the physical activity of running, there is something else going on. St Paul in the New Testament often likens the Christian life to running a race. In his letter to the Timothy he writes, *I have fought the good fight, I have finished the race, I have kept the faith* (2 Timothy, 4:7).

In his letter to the Galatians Paul writes, *in order to make sure that I was not running, or had not run, in vain.* (Gal. 2:2)

A few chapters later we find the words:

You were running well; who prevented you from obeying the truth? (Gal. 5:7)

In his letter to the Corinthians we find the following verses:

Do you not know that in a race the runners all compete, but only one receives the Prize? Run in such a way that you may win it. Athletes exercise self-control in all things: they do it to receive a perishable garland, but we an imperishable one. So I do not run aimlessly, nor do I box as though beating the air, but I punish my body and enslave it, so that after proclaiming to others, I myself should not be disqualified. (1 Cor. 9: 24–27)

Finally, the writer to the Hebrews says:

Therefore, since we are surrounded by so great a cloud of witnesses, let us lay aside every weight and sin that clings so closely, and let us run with perseverance the race that is set before us, looking to Jesus the pioneer and perfected of our faith. (Hebs.12: 1, 2)

Clearly, these authors are not talking about literally running a race but about running the race of life. I wonder why they use the metaphor of running rather than, say, walking or strolling. Clearly, some people seem to stroll through life without a care in the world, but most of the people I know have some kind of burden, hardship or misfortune in their lives that they have to deal with. My life has been no exception. Of course, there have been times when life has been full of fun and enjoyment. Other times have been much less so. There was the occasion when my Mum rang up to say that Dad had died very suddenly; when my sister rang to say her grandson had a cerebral tumour; when my marriage went through a very difficult time and we decided to call it a day after nearly 25 years; not to mention the many ups and downs of daily life ministering to a congregation.

That is why the metaphor of running is used; because running, as opposed to just walking, requires a deal of energy and effort, as does living with our particular problems or difficulties. Some days the going is tough and some days it feels a bit easier. Some days, life requires a deal of perseverance. If we are going to get anywhere at all, we need a lot of self-control and discipline. Victoria Pendleton, the cyclist and Olympic gold medalist, in a recent interview pointed out the similarities between sport and religion. 'It requires discipline and focus and it encourages an honest and pure kind of living. As with most religious faiths, you put in the effort, follow the guidelines and reach something greater.'(*The Observer*, 21.6.14)

Consequently, this book attempts to draw some parallels with running and the Christian life. There are even exercises at the end of each chapter. There is also something to ponder. You may be tempted to keep turning the pages of this book. Please note; it is not a race. Spend time on the exercise and take time to ponder. Hopefully, you will also reflect on how the each chapter relates to your life. The key task is to relate what is said to *your* life. *Your* life is the important one.

Chapter 1

Y?

Why? 'Why is that man running?' the little boy asked his mum. I didn't wait to hear her reply. I wonder what she would have said if she knew I was training for a marathon! Why on earth did I want to run a marathon especially since I have reached the biblical age of three score years and ten! This is the age when some people are thinking about taking things easy – a gentle walk round the park, a few holes on the golf course, pottering around the garden or pushing the swing for the grandchild. It's the time of life when the rot begins to set in. You get to the top of the stairs and wonder what you went up the stairs for. You have completely forgotten. Those senior moments become more frequent. Things begin to ache a little more, or fall out, or wrinkle. I don't mind being called an old wrinkly but I draw the line at an old crumbly.

The answer to the little boy's question is not easy to find. Was it my last effort to fight against the ravages of time and show the world that there is still some life left in the old dog? God has not finished with me yet. Was it an attempt to show that 70 is the new 50? After all, that is what I feel like – most of the time. Was it because I like to respond to a challenge which seems a little bit more than I can chew? There's the old saying – 'your reach has got to exceed your grasp'. I remember jumping in at the deep end when I went on a 30-day silent retreat.[1] It was something I thought I would never be able to do, but it was a never-to-be-forgotten experience. Could it have been that I liked physical exercise and the feeling of physical well-being? 'Mens sana in corpora sano' – a healthy mind in a healthy body. Maybe I was all too aware that I was beginning to put on weight and needed to take drastic action in order to be more sylph-like. Oh the chance would be a fine thing!

If you really want to know my physical attributes, I am actually a tiny shade under six foot and weigh fourteen and a half stone – not exactly built for running. Happily, since running, my waist has shrunk by four inches but my weight has not changed much. My story is that muscles weigh more than fat and so that is what I am sticking with, but I just do not like too much fat. For some people it doesn't seem to be a problem. Having just returned from a sun-drenched beach on the island of Rhodes, quite a number of people were literally letting it all hang out and droop down. In truth, they looked like beached whales but they didn't seem to care at all. Maybe I'm a bit narcissistic so I'll just have to not look in any pools of water. Narcissus, you remember, was the Greek God who fell in love with himself. The story goes that when he saw his own reflection in a pool of water he was completely enamored with it, but committed suicide when he realised he couldn't have the object of his affections.

Vanities of vanities! All is vanity. (Eccl. 1:1)

Actually, I think our bodies are very important and we neglect them or misuse them at our peril. Traditionally,

5

Christianity has been a bit uncomfortable with bodies. Body became associated with flesh in early Christianity and there was a separation between the things of the spirit and the things of the flesh; the former being on a far higher plane than the latter. This distinction mirrored the Greek division into body and soul. People have been suspicious of bodily pleasures, let alone more explicit sexual pleasures. To imagine sex as a joyous act would have been anathema to, for example, the Puritans and the Victorians. Interestingly, Jesus comes in the form of a human body. That is what Christmas is all about, the love of God becoming incarnate in the world. As the fourth gospel puts it, *'the Word became flesh and lived among us.'* (John, 1:14)

Barbara Brown Taylor has a chapter on this theme in her recent book.[2] She writes about the practice of wearing skin and, in particular, those times when we are fed up with our bodies. If you are full of loathing for your body, she recommends that you 'pray naked in front of a full-length mirror... Maybe you think you are too heavy. Maybe you have never liked the way your hipbones stick out. Do your breasts sag? Are you too hairy? ...Maybe you have come through some surgery that has changed the way you look... Whether you are sick or well, lovely or irregular, there comes a time when it is vitally important for your spiritual health to drop your clothes, look in the mirror, and say, "Here I am. This is the body-like-no-other that my life has shaped. I live here. This is my soul's address".'[3] There is a lot to be thankful for. I am acutely aware of this whenever I think of my friend Andy.

Andy is a similar age to me but there is a major difference in our lives. He has been in a wheelchair all his life. Not only that, he has no muscular usage at all, except for his tongue. He can speak but that is about all. He controls his mobility chair, and electrical things in his home, with an array of buttons, which he moves with his tongue. In spite of all this, he is a lovely Christian person with a great sense of humour. Why should I complain with my petty aches and pains?

Running is a way of saying thank you that my body is more or less in working order. In my early days as a minister, there was a church member who was always telling anecdotes. I remember the following one in particular.

Blind man: 'If only I could see again, I would give thanks to God.' Minister: 'Did you when you could?'

Some people say that if you can't think of anything else to say in your prayers, then at least say 'thank you.' Running has become my way of expressing gratitude.

A further reason for running is that I know exercise, as well as diet, can reduce the chances of incurring type two diabetes and since my dad had that very same, it gave me some serious food for thought. He had to inject himself every day and if I can do anything to prevent that happening then I will do it. Needles and I are not a good mixture. The hidden agenda was that if I did a certain amount of exercise, maybe I could allow myself a little bit of chocolate as well, even if I had been diagnosed as having impaired glucose intolerance. There is method in the madness after all! It may be a combination of all these factors but I suspect that the roots of my motivation lie in the dim and distant past.

Whilst in the fifth form (Year 11) at Bolton school, I was persuaded, cajoled, volunteered into running a cross-country so that my House could gain a few more points. I went round the course with a sixth former who offered help, advice and encouragement, but what an effort it was. I discovered muscles where before there had been nothing that I was aware of. I climbed the stairs at home as though I had an elephant in each pocket. Most definitely this was a one-off experience. I simply did not have the physique or the inclination to be a cross-country runner. Some people are lean and lithe and just born to be athletic, others are more muscular and born for some kind of impact sport. I rapidly came to the conclusion that I was born to sit and think – and sometimes just to sit.

To add insult to injury, round about the same time as this brief exploration into cross-country territory, my P.E. teacher introduced me to the joys of circuit training! Yet more muscles introduced themselves in unexpected places. The strange thing is that I took a kind of sadistic pleasure in lifting weights! Not, let me tell you, that I was any good at it, but there was something good about having tighter muscles rather than a lot of jelly-like flab. Is this very narcissistic?

The only other thing remotely connected to this is when in my mid-teens I, and some friends, climbed Mount Snowdon in North Wales. For some silly reason we decided to run all the way down the Ranger track. I seem to remember doing it in about 30 minutes but then it was downhill all the way! Please note that this time may be wrong; memory has an unfortunate knack of distorting the truth.

Many years later, I watched the first London marathon on the television. As I sat glued to the television (before going to church!), a small spark of something was ignited within me. Perhaps I could do that one day. Of course, this feeling was aided by the fact that the beginning of the race took place in Greenwich Park. As a student I used to live near to the park, just across Blackheath, and I often walked around it, especially at the time of examinations. Sometimes, I vaguely remember, I even had a young lady in tow. Who would have imagined in their wildest dreams that one day I would be starting a marathon from that very same park 50 years later?

The other contributory factor happened about 20 years ago. The Methodist church developed the wonderful policy of awarding their ministers the gift of a three-month sabbatical after a certain length of service. I was eligible. During the first month I gradually became aware of the fact that I was sitting in front of my computer rather a lot and, as a result, was beginning to put on weight and feel very lethargic. What was the solution? I started to go for little jogs. Not long ones, you understand, just little ones round where I lived in Dorking. The result was that I started to feel a lot better. Some years later, on moving to Petersfield in Hampshire, there was an ideal place to go for the occasional jog and so I did. It worked wonders. I was away from the study and the telephone, and all the demands of ministry seemed to take on a new perspective as I did this exercise. Not only that, I actually felt much better.

Round about the same time, my family bought me a surprise present – a bench for lifting weights. I had dabbled in weight training now and again but hadn't really taken it seriously since school days 50 years earlier. Now I had a bench. There was no excuse and no escape.

Time rolled on, as it does, and I finally retired to Portchester. As luck would have it, we found a house within two minutes of the sea shore. What a wonderful place to go for a jog: no traffic, no roads, no concrete, just a grass verge and plenty of fresh air. There was really no excuse. Moreover, I now had the time to do some serious training. After a couple of years I felt ready for a serious challenge and so I entered for the Great South Run in Portsmouth, just down the road from where I live. What could be easier? For reasons unknown, except the usual one of a computer glitch, I thought I had entered, but in fact my name hadn't been registered. Disappointment set in, but nothing ventured, nothing gained; I decided to run 10 miles round about where I live. My wife was the only spectator and encourager, but she was enough. I completed my first 10 miles all by myself. To say I was tired would be an understatement. The only thing that made me get out of a long hot bath was the smell of food wafting up from the kitchen.

My next challenge was the Portsmouth half marathon some months later. I have to admit this was a far more daunting prospect. Not only was it my first experience at that distance, it was also my first experience of running alongside other people. Of course, most of them passed me in the first few minutes. All I could hear was the patter of countless numbers of feet. Of course, it was a completely different experience to running on one's own. For a start, you had to concentrate so as not to run into anybody else, or suddenly change course, thereby, confusing the person behind. Coming towards the end of this race my legs felt like jelly. A lady who was considerably younger than me shouted out rather unkindly for all to hear, 'You're supposed to be running not walking.' I could hardly move but, somehow, I managed to complete the course. My mind went back to the scene of a well-known marathon runner, Jim Peters, actually failing to reach the finishing line. He was the first man to clock a marathon in under two hours twenty minutes, but at the Vancouver Commonwealth Games in 1954, although he reached the stadium 17 minutes ahead of the next runner, it took him 11 minutes to run another 200 metres. I vividly remember seeing him on the television. He wobbled and wobbled and eventually he collapsed and fell to the ground. He had to be carried out of the stadium on a stretcher without having completed the course.

As a result of my experience, the realisation hit me that if I was going to take this running business seriously, I really needed to get some help. I purchased a book by Paula Radcliffe and immediately discovered that I had not been doing things quite right.[4] My training really needed to improve and so did my diet. I had run the half marathon with very little idea of what I was doing. For example, it never occurred to me that it would help if I ate a few more carbohydrates for my breakfast, not to mention an energy bar. The only thing I ensured was that I drank enough liquid on my way round. This was a lesson I had learned the hard way.

Later in the year another chance came to enter for the Great South Run and this time I was successful. I was quite excited about this because it was less of a serious occasion with more 'fun' runners taking part. Not only that, it was 4.1 miles less than the Half, so what did I have to worry about? This was going to be a doddle. That wasn't exactly the case. The head wind along the coast was fearsome. Walking, at times, was the only solution and so my time was a little slower than expected. However, still feeling there was a little energy left, I decided to run home – another eight miles! Amazingly, I just about made it, with a little walking on the way and my wife placed at strategic intervals with some much needed liquid.

Having completed 18 miles, albeit quite slowly, I dared to think that maybe, just maybe, the London Marathon was becoming a distinct possibility. Some of my friends thought I was stark raving bonkers to even think about it, whilst others were just too polite to say so. 'You know you are a runner when your family and friends pretend to understand you, but really think you are mad and should be committed.'[5]

In fairness, some were worried about my health: 'You can't do that at your age.' 'You can't be serious, what about your knees and your hips?' Others were quick to inform me that it was a bit further than half a marathon. Being a former mathematics teacher, I was able to say that it was actually twice as far – 26.2 miles! Notwithstanding all the discouraging comments, I took the plunge and entered for the London Marathon of 2014. I entered through the charity 'Help the Hospices', but imagine my disappointment when they refused my entry. I was distraught. Was somebody trying to tell me something? Anyway, I don't easily give up and so I applied again and gave in depth reasons for wanting to support this particular charity. I was accepted! What joy! I was over the moon. I was actually entered for the London Marathon 2014. It was sometime later before reality began to seep through and I began to realise the enormity of what I had undertaken. This was September 2013 and the race was in April the following year. That gave me a little over seven months to get to grips with Paula Radcliffe's book and do some serious work. The next few months looked daunting. There was a mountain to climb. I needed to do some very serious training.

Exercise:

I'll find a piece of paper and write down all the things I am thankful for.

To Ponder:

This chapter is headed 'why?' and leads to *the* ultimate question, why is there anything here at all? Scientists are busy answering how the universe came into existence – the Big Bang and all that – but there remains the unanswered question. Why is there anything here at all?

Chapter 2

Training

Black toes! One of the early lessons to learn is that if your running shoes are not correctly fitted, you very soon end up with black toes caused by blood blisters under the nails. They don't look very pleasant at all. It is, therefore, very important to go to a sports shop to get the right kind of footwear. Paula Radcliffe even has a section in her book on the anatomy of a running shoe! In a good sports shop you will be introduced to 'pronation', which is the inward roll of the foot whilst running or walking. You can be a neutral runner, an overpronator or a supinator. Here's me thinking that running was simply a matter of putting one foot in front of the other as fast as you can for as long as you can! Believe me; it is worth the effort – and the cost! – to buy the right kind of foot wear. Did you know that each foot has 26 bones, 33 joints, 107 ligaments and 19 muscles and tendons? All this complex anatomy deserves due care and attention and running becomes so much easier without blisters and other nasties to contend with. Of course, there is a simple requirement that helps one to avoid black toes; that is keeping one's nails short and a liberal supply of Vaseline.

Another interesting word I came across was 'cadence', that is, the number of steps you take per minute. The higher your cadence, the less contact with the ground, less energy is absorbed by the ground and so, theoretically, you will run faster. This is all very well in theory but I'm afraid whatever happens I find it difficult to run very fast. Indeed, I'm quite sure that some people walk faster than I run. Length of stride may well be important, but if my stride was any shorter I would meet myself coming back.

Then there is the question of what to wear. This might seem all too obvious but the wrong vest, underwear or shorts can lead to chaffing and that is not very pleasant. Furthermore, you might need different attire depending on the weather conditions. There is also the question of what variety of socks to wear. You thought that all you had to do was put on any old clothes and off you go. Oh, dear me, no. I'm afraid not. In one sense, running is undemanding in that you don't need very much kit, but it is very important to have the *correct* kit.

Even when you are correctly kitted out and raring to go, it is a whole new agenda to look at your diet! This would require a chapter, if not a book on its own, so suffice it to say that it is important what one eats, especially in the days immediately before a long race. Food provides the energy, the fuel for the run and so it is helpful to eat the right stuff. I found, for example, that on the odd occasion I ate fish and chips, running the day after was not a good idea. I seemed to be full of wind – more than usual that is. Try filling a diesel engine with petrol and see how far you get! On second thoughts, don't try because you will ruin the engine.

In one sense, running is just about putting one foot in front of the other. However, if you are really going to improve then it is a good idea to have a stopwatch to keep a check on your time. This might seem almost an unnecessary thing to do, but often I have felt it was not a very good run and yet found that my time was better than I had thought. The reverse was also the case. Thinking I had had a good run I was disappointed to discover that my stopwatch was telling a different story. It is much better to rely on an objective measure of one's training than on purely subjective feelings.

I began running quite a small distance and slowly, very slowly, increasing it by running to the next lamppost. Actually, in my case it was the next boat. I am fortunate enough to live very close to the sea and so I can run along the seashore without any fear of traffic or air pollution or too many people. Then, it is a good idea to vary one's routine – mixing up your speed by running a bit faster and then slower, sometimes a short run, sometimes a long run and some uphill running. Believe it or not, I actually used to run up a hill – quite slowly. We live very near to the South Downs. Not that I ran to the top. I managed to run up about a third of a very small foothill known as Portsdown Hill.

The recommendation is that you also do some weight training. Happy memories. This is to strengthen your muscles and general resilience. I was introduced to 'wonderful' exercises like the plank, the bridge, the foot glide, kettle swings and a single-leg Russian deadlift! I found exercises for the upper body, the feet and proprioception (balance), the hip (piriformis) muscle (the piriformis muscle controls the outward rotation of your hip) and peroneal exercises (there are three peroneus muscles in your lower leg). You live and learn! In addition, there is a hip bridge, Russian twists, lunges, squats, side walking lunges, walking knee raise, bum kicks and many, many more. When reading about all this it was like a textbook on medieval torture. All that's missing was the rack, the thumb screw and the water torture.

The theory behind all these exercises is that in running you use your whole body, not just your feet and legs and the stronger you are the more able you will be to complete the distance. In the process, I discovered that apart from the more well-known things like hamstrings and Achilles tendon, I also had quads and glutes. This was a whole new world of unexplored territory for me. Not only was I learning about my body, I was extending my vocabulary and getting as fit as a fiddle into the bargain. On second thoughts, as fit as a fiddle that needed a lot of tuning.

I never used to look forward to Tuesdays because that was the day I had my long run. Paula Radcliffe says one of the prerequisites is that you should enjoy running. Try as I might, I never enjoyed Tuesdays. It was a day to be endured rather than enjoyed. I actually used to run on circular routes that always included my house. This was absolutely vital for water breaks and, sometimes, loo breaks. It also meant that I sometimes passed the same pedestrian twice: 'Are you still running?' 'Have I just seen your brother?'

Of course, the best day of the week was Sunday, my day of rest. Paula says that recovery days are not optional. I took her at her word. In fact, I decided to make allowances for my age and took two days off. What bliss. I could laze around without feeling guilty! A lovely little book that was actually written for children is entitled 'Jesus' day off'.[6] It takes about two minutes to read but it's worth it, not only for the content, but also for the pictures. There is some wisdom in the Old Testament idea of taking one day a week off from all one's normal duties. Time to rest, chill out, relax, get things in perspective and have some fun.

Six days you shall labour and do all your work, but the seventh day is a Sabbath to the Lord your God. On it you shall not do any work. (Exodus, 20:9)

Sadly, in our culture, we have lost this rhythm of work and play. For many it is all work and little quality time for relaxation. According to the book of Genesis, even God had a rest on the seventh day of creation.

By the seventh day God had finished the work he had been doing; so on the seventh day he rested from all his work. And God blessed the seventh day and made it holy, because he rested from all the work of creating that he had done. (Genesis, 2:2)

One of the benefits of being retired is that I could actually choose when to go for a run. If the weather was inclement, for example raining, I could always wait in the hope that it would pass over. However, the winter of 2013–14 was very wet and the nationwide floods were a testimony to that fact. My fair-weather running sometimes had to be forsworn if I was to do any running at all. The drawback of my particular training run is that there was more often than not, a breeze coming off the sea. Funnily enough, whichever way I ran the wind always seemed to be against me! In other words, training was a great effort. One is supposed to enjoy the experience but for me it was more like gritting my teeth and enduring it. On one occasion, a man was coming in the opposite way and as he passed he said, 'Look as though you are enjoying it.' From then on I tried to smile at people but I fear it was more of a grimace.

That comment leads me to thinking about the Christian life. I wonder why it is that Christians often don't seem to be enjoying themselves. After all, joy is one of the fruits of the Spirit (Gal. 5:22), so why do many not seem to be full of this particular fruit. My guess is that we often hit the spiritual wall, but there will be more of this in chapter four. The fruit goes rotten and there is a discrepancy between what people think and what they feel. Another reason, maybe, is that we spend time doing things that are deadening rather than life-inducing. If there is one thing the gospel is about, it is about Life with a capital 'L'.

I am the bread of life. (John, 6:35)

The thief comes only to steal and kill and destroy. I come that they may have life and have it abundantly. (John, 10:10)

I am the resurrection and the life. (John, 11:25)

These are all words coming out of the mouth of Jesus. What could be plainer? The gospel is about Life. Are you doing things that energise you and bring you to life? If so, I will stick my neck out and say they come from God. God is a God of Life. If you are doing things that have the opposite effect, ask yourself why.

Let me return to training. Two things are essential: a warm up and a warm down. I confess to having heard of the former but not the latter. When I went on my first cross-country run at school all those years ago, I'm certain there was no mention of a warm down. In fact, I don't even remember having a shower. All I did was change and catch the bus home. No wonder I was so stiff the day after! A warm up and a warm down are both essential. The warm up is to reduce the chances of pulling a muscle or some other injury. The warm down consists of lots of stretching exercises to restrict stiffness.

In spite of all the training and all the precautions, unexpected things can still happen. The picture of Paula Radcliffe in tears at an Athens roadside during the Olympics was very poignant. In spite of all the hard work, the training, the preparation, something went wrong and she could not complete her marathon run. There was no obvious explanation as to why this should happen to such a superb athlete and world record holder.

Sometimes things happen to us in the Christian life to which there is no obvious explanation. We say our prayers, read the bible, go to church and generally try to lead a Christian life but then we are hit in the solar plexus. Tragedy strikes and it comes unexpectedly. Christians are not immune from the vagaries of life. Indeed, it seems sometimes that 'as flies to wanton boys are we to the Gods. They kill us for their sport' (*King Lear*, Shakespeare.). These words are uttered by Gloucester as he wanders on the heath. He is blind and homeless and on the point of entrusting himself to an apparently half-mad beggar. Contrast these words of despair with the classic biblical example of undeserved suffering.

This is to be found in the Old Testament in the book of Job. You will remember that Job loses just about everything – he lost his health, his family, his cattle, his servants, just about all it is possible to lose and yet *'he is blameless and upright, a man who fears God and shuns evil.'* (Job, 1:8)

Sometimes there are no answers to much of what happens to us. For some the effect is no longer to believe in God. Their faith is shattered. For others, it is precisely when the chips are down that they stick with it and discover that God is taking them to a deeper, richer faith. Job, in spite of all, continued to hope and believe in God.

I know that my Redeemer lives, and that in the end he will stand upon the earth. And after my skin has been destroyed,
yet in my flesh I will see God: I myself will see him, with my own eyes – I, and not another.
How my heart yearns within me! (Job, 19: 25–27)

19

What a wonderful affirmation that is. In spite of all his afflictions, Job is still able to say, 'I know that my Redeemer lives.' What a great statement of faith.

One thing became clear to me during training, that it is very important to set goals. The short-term goal might be to run a little faster or a little further than last time. The long-term goal was the London marathon. If I hadn't had that to aim for, all the tea in China would not have persuaded me to go out running on a cold, wet and windy winter's day. Believe you me, having something to aim for provided a lot of motivation. Without that goal it would have been very tempting to give up and opt for a less strenuous life. If there is no destination, then how do we know when we have arrived? A boat that has not set a course will simply drift on the tide or be at the mercy of any prevailing winds. This brings me to the matter of distractions.

Exercise:

What are the short-term goals in my life?

What are my long-term goals in my life? Are they realistic or merely a pipe dream?

What do I need to do to ensure that I achieve my goals? What do I find helpful or less helpful in achieving my goals?

What might God be asking me to do? Or be?

To ponder:

How do I spend my time? Am I doing things that are life-giving or that are deadening?

Which are the ones that energise me and fill me with joy and a zest for life?

Chapter 3

Distractions

Dogs! I fear, dear reader, that this might be a rant against your best friend, a dog, but I have to say that they can be a very serious distraction when running. To be fair, some owners are very good and have even been known to distract their dog with some food when they see me coming. Others are less considerate. When a dog jumps up at me, a typical response from the owner might be, 'Oh, you are a naughty dog, a very naughty dog,' or 'I'm sorry but he doesn't like runners.' On one memorable occasion a great dane jumped up at me and very nearly knocked me off my feet. Many, many times the owner has been completely unaware of the fact that their four-footed friend is blocking the pathway and therefore make no effort to bring it to heel. Frequently I have had to stop dead in my tracks and make way for their dog, which obviously doesn't know any better since it hasn't been properly trained.

'Hector, come here.' 'Hector, come here, *now*.' The final command is said in a plaintive, pleading voice. 'Hector, pleeeeeeeeeeeeeeeeeeeeeeeeeeeeease come here.' More by good luck than by good training the dog slowly retreats to its owner. 'Phoebe, don't jump up', 'No, Phoebe, *don't* do that', 'Phoebe, pleeeeeeeeeeeeeeeeeeeeeeeeeeeeease don't do that.' These are genuine remarks that I have heard. The 'please' is the only word I have introduced. As if to add insult to injury, that is, a scratched leg, nine times out of ten there is no apology. In fairness, I have to say that there are some 'good dogs' and some good owners.

My main objection is when animals, in particular, dogs, are treated as though they are human. I'm all for taking care of God's creatures and, indeed, enjoying them, but in the last analysis they are not human. They have different needs and behaviours and they do need to be trained, usually to one-word commands. Just to put the record straight, we did have a dog in our household for a few years. It is a great joy to be welcomed in the morning and when coming in from work to be greeted by a four-legged friend who rolls over on his back and shrieks with joy at seeing you. Nobody else does that. The pure unconditional acceptance and delight are so uplifting. Amazing though it may seem, I believe that God has exactly the same attitude towards us. God delights in our presence even though he might say, 'I've not seen you for some time!' and God's love is absolutely unconditional.

If there is one parable that summarises the gospel, it is the parable of the prodigal son in Luke's gospel chapter 15. If ever there was a lost son, here he is. Not only is he found to be eating with pigs, which were considered to be unclean by Jews, he is in a foreign land and squandered all his wealth. Eventually he *came to himself* and decided things would be much better at home. Would you believe it? His father is actually looking out for him. Not only that, he gives him shoes and a cloak and throws a banquet, all before the son has had the change to say he is sorry. The love of the father is truly amazing.

The object of going on a silent retreat is that distractions are reduced to an absolute minimum and so there is actually more space for God. There is no conversation, no music or reading, no post or telephone, no television or radio and, hopefully, no mobile phone. Not only have I lived through a 30-day silent retreat and can testify to the power of silence, but I have also facilitated many silent retreats for other people. Participants turn up full of worries, tired and generally stressed out. Even after just one weekend of silence they return home literally buzzing. God has found them in their silence. It is true. I am not making this up. Words so often get in the way. They can act as a barrier. Church services often come over as a plethora of words and, I think, God is often kept out. There is no way in. Our silence, at least, offers God a chance to say something.

Other major distractions occurred before I even changed into my kit! One glance out of the window would persuade me that the weather just wasn't suitable for running and so I used to find all sorts of jobs that needed to be done right there and then; anything to keep me indoors in my comfort zone. The need to ring somebody up suddenly would become very urgent. There would be some e-mails that really needed responding to... The hoovering needed to be done. Yes, really. Of course, I had to check out what was happening in the News, just in case something important was happening that could possibly have an immediate effect on me. I'd better pay that electric bill before I forget. These, and hundreds of other petty things, needed to be done there and then.

I started to reflect that sometimes finding time to pray is a bit like that. It is all too easy to find excuses for not spending time with God. There is always so much to *do*. Some people have long lists of things that need to be done and so rarely get time just to *be* without feeling enormously guilty. There is a great pressure in our society to prove yourself and very often the first question one is asked in a conversation is 'What do you do?' Imagine the response if the answer was, 'I've just spent half an hour praying.'

All this resistance is very strange and paradoxical because we know for sure that God is a God of love. In fact, that is the only definition of God in the New Testament.

'God is love.' (1 John, 4:16)

Why then do we resist coming into the presence of God? Is it awe? Is it fear? Is it some hidden secret that God might find out about us? Is it that we simply can't be bothered? All this praying business, indeed, religion, is a complete waste of time – especially when there is so much to do.

There is a very good biblical example in the gospel of Luke. This is an incident when Jesus is at the home of Martha and Mary. Martha is in the kitchen, presumably with plenty to do preparing a meal or some such for her guests, whilst Mary simply sits at the feet of Jesus listening to what he has to say. Martha was somewhat resentful of her sister. She was *'distracted by all the preparations that had to be made.'* She went to Jesus and said, *'Lord, don't you care that my sister has left me to do the work all by myself? Tell her to help me!'*

That seems to me to be a very reasonable request but the answer of Jesus was, *'Martha, Martha, you are worried and upset about many things, but only one thing is needed. Mary has chosen what is better, and it will not be taken away from her.'* (Luke, 10: 38–42)

That is a very surprising answer. No sympathy at all for Martha. The reality is that there is a bit of Martha and Mary in all of us and the challenge is to find the balance between the doing and the being. When things get out of kilter we can find ourselves totally stressed out and on the way to a burn out or, in running terms, we can hit the wall. On the other hand, we can spend so much time 'being', that nothing at all gets done. As the old expression has it, 'don't be so heavenly-minded that you are no earthly good'. I shall be saying more about finding space in the next chapter.

An important distraction is pain, that is, when the body is trying to tell you something. It is very difficult to concentrate on anything when you are in pain. I remember as a teenager being doubled up with toothache. The whole of my head seemed to be throbbing. I have great sympathy for those who suffer from migraine. The ultimate distraction in running is some kind of injury. On one occasion, after a long run, I awoke in the middle of the night with an excruciating pain in my right shin. I had the dreaded shin splints. This is an inflammation of the tendon on the outer edge of the tibia, which is the bone at the front of the lower leg. It usually arises out of too much training and the impact of repeated landings on hard surfaces. All I know is that it was very, very painful. Indeed, to such an extent that I resorted to painkillers, I think for the first time since I had that serious toothache.

Luckily, there is a sports clinic nearby in Portsmouth and so I was able to get some advice and good massage from the lovely physiotherapist, Louise. From then on, Lucy, my even lovelier wife, kindly gave me some shin massages every day up to the big day. Consequently, I was able to return to training after a two-week break. The moral of the story is that when there is a major distraction like this, it has to be dealt with. In a similar way, if we are trying to focus on something, whatever it is, and we keep getting distracted, then it is prudent to deal with the distraction.

There are other injuries related to running like stress fractures, blisters, chafing, athlete's foot, Achilles tendonitis, pulled hamstring, plantar fasciitis (a painful stress of the heel bone). Fortunately, I didn't suffer from any of these, not even cramp. This is caused by poor food and hydration management – depleted magnesium, sodium or potassium levels – so I can only infer that my diet was up to standard. Sometimes, I developed the common or garden stitch. This is caused by fast, shallow, or irregular breathing and can usually be alleviated by deep, regular breathing.

Soon after I retired, when I began jogging a bit more, I tripped up and broke a rib. There was nothing that could be done except an enforced rest for about six weeks. A couple of years after that, I developed a really nasty abscess on my backside. Please note, dear reader, that I have heard all the jokes about bottoms, backsides and rears. Anyway, the bottom line (!) is that surgery was required. Actually, it was the first time in my life I had had a general anaesthetic and it was quite an experience. You are handed over to people you have never met and they are usually from different parts of the world, you very quickly go to sleep and then, after never having felt a thing, you wake up in a different place. I imagine dying to be something like this – handing yourself over to someone, going to sleep and then waking up in another place. Of course, after the operation I was out of action for another few weeks. Yet another minor ailment happened about a year later when I developed a nasty infection under one of my big toes. At least that was the initial diagnosis. Imagine the disbelief of nurses and doctors when they discovered maggots there! Yes, maggots! It was so unusual the nurse asked to take a video for teaching purposes. My big toe became famous! The upshot was I had another anaesthetic to remove my nail and consequently I had to take another few weeks without exercise.

I relate these incidents to indicate that distractions happen and they have to be taken into consideration. More insidious are the distractions that are internal. That voice, which can sometimes be very insistent, says things like, 'This is a silly idea going out for a run, why not stay in where it's nice and warm.' 'You really shouldn't be doing this at your age.' 'You must be absolutely bonkers.' 'Why not do something more fruitful and leisurely like write a book.' 'I think you need to spend a bit more time with your wife.' Actually this last temptation wasn't too strong because I was able to run twice a week when Lucy, my wife, was working. However, the other inner voices were very strong and persistent. As already mentioned, there were the outer voices as well. 'You must be mad.' 'I don't usually sponsor insanity.' There were not many voices that I can recall which actually encouraged me to carry on.

Even louder are the inner voices, which shout at you when you are actually running and things are not going too well, you just don't feel like it or the weather is inclement. 'I think you've done enough for today, why not pack it in and run home?' 'You must be mad running in this weather.' 'I don't think my body can take much more of this.' 'O God, why don't you send a lot of traffic along the road so I won't be able to cross over and I can have a nice long rest.' Yes, I have actually heard all these voices including the last one but, of course, God doesn't work like that. God is not there just to answer all my little whims. Much as we might like it, God is not Father Christmas providing us with lots of lovely presents. God loves us far too much and knows us far too well to give us just what we want. Moreover, if I need a rest, why do I need God to provide it for me? Am I not able to take a rest for myself? As somebody once said, God doesn't do for us what we are entirely capable of doing for ourselves. That is the danger of prayer. If you ask God to do something, the answer might well be, 'Why don't you do something about it yourself?'

Sometimes we have to do things because we believe that it is the right course of action for us, even though other people may think otherwise. This is a very difficult road to pursue because sometimes the other people can be right! One can come across as very stubborn and pig-headed. I guess the only antidote to this is to gradually test the waters and build up slowly. In other words, not to go headlong into a full marathon without first ensuring that your body can cope with the demands and stresses. Listening to your own body is very important. For example, if you have an injury or a niggle somewhere, the last thing you want to do is to make it worse by going out for a run. Even this can be a pitfall. Have I really got a niggle or am I just wanting to get out of a run?

It occurs to me that many of these distractions, or inner voices, occur when we pray, but first a look at something which can happen to all athletes whatever level of fitness they have reached.

Exercise:

I'm starting to imagine that I'm looking at the shape of a heart. This heart grows and grows and grows. It is becoming so large I cannot see when it starts and where it ends. Slowly this heart enfolds me and I can relax in its presence. What am I feeling?

To Ponder:

What is the purpose of life? Is there any purpose at all?

Have I set a 'course' for my life or am I drifting along?

What are the things that distract and divert me from doing what I would really like to do?

Chapter 4

The Wall

Berlin. This was not just any wall, it was the Berlin Wall with a capital 'B' and capital 'W' and I hit it! Very hard. After about 17 miles, whilst going round the St Catherine's Dock area, my energy levels plummeted and everything began to hurt. When I say everything that is exactly what I mean. The following words were found on Google and they summarise precisely how I felt:

'At mile 20 I thought I was dead.

At mile 22 I wished I was dead.

At mile 24 I knew I was dead.

At mile 26.2 I realised I had become too tough to kill.'

My condition wasn't helped by the fact that for some strange reason I missed a water station.

At least it felt as though I had and so I hit the wall. The wall is the point in the marathon when a runner's glycogen, that is stored energy within the muscles, is depleted and you are forced to slow down considerably and in some cases, as in mine, just walk for a little while. All you can do is keep going putting one foot in front of the other in the hope that some energy will return. Some people call it 'getting your second wind'. My second wind never seemed to come. In fact, it felt as though I kept hitting the wall. I was, literally, running on empty even though I had taken some precautions.

One of the recommendations to avoid hitting the wall is to do progressively longer runs each week. This means that the muscles' capacity to store more glycogen increases. In addition, the long runs teach the body to tap into and utilize energy reserves from fat storage sites after the glycogen stores have been depleted. I tried to run a little bit further every week in my training. In addition, so the traditional advice goes, you have to run a 20 mile training run so that your body adjusts to storing glycogen and uses it when necessary. Happily, the advice is not to run more than 20 miles otherwise there may be some potential negative effects, which outweigh the positive ones. There was never any danger of me running more than one 20 miler, but I did manage one. That was more than enough!

The other piece of advice is not to start a marathon too quickly. If you start the marathon too quickly you run the risk of burning up your stored energy too quickly, so you get tired more quickly and hence you 'crash' and hit the wall. Being all too aware of this advice, I began quite slowly but it didn't prevent the inevitable.

I wonder what you do if you hit the wall during your spiritual life. I say 'if' you hit the wall, but in all probability it is 'when' you hit the wall. If you ever find the time to pray, there are those nagging voices inside: 'Why bother, praying is a waste of time' 'I don't think there is a God anyway' 'Why does God never seem to answer my prayers?' 'I really can't afford the time, there is so much that I have to do.' On the other hand, we might be feeling tired, bored or fed up because nothing that we do seems to be bringing us closer to God. Indeed, the opposite seems to be happening. However much we try, and however many words we use, there doesn't seem to be any positive effect. Our spiritual energy begins to run out and our batteries seem to be empty. A good symptom of this is if you find yourself singing a hymn, or saying the words of a familiar prayer, and your heart is in a completely different place to your head. Well, of course it is, but that's not the point; I mean metaphorically not literally!

These are the internal voices, but there are also external influences, which affect our spiritual life. It is nigh on impossible to concentrate on anything, let alone prayer, if you are suffering from a pain like toothache. If you are in a stressful situation, for example, at work, or you are going through a relationship problem or there has been a bereavement amongst your nearest and dearest; these can all have an adverse effect on our prayer life. Then there are actual external noises. The children are being particularly boisterous, the television is on, the neighbour is cutting his lawn, there is a lot of traffic on the road and even the aeroplanes seem to be more frequent than usual. Everything seems to be working against you.

The other thing that works against us finding time for prayer is our busyness. Mike Yaconelli in a book called *Messy Spirituality* writes, 'It's not that we're too decadent, we're too busy. We don't feel guilty because of sin, but because we have no time for our spouse, our children or our God. It's not sinning too much that's killing our souls, it's our schedule that's annihilating us... Spiritual growth is not 'running faster', as in more meetings, more bible studies and more prayer meetings. Spiritual growth happens when we slow our activity down, not when we increase it. If we want to meet Jesus, we can't do it on the run.'[7]

What can you do?

It takes time. You can't be busy and pray at the same time. You can be active and pray, you can work and pray, but you can't be busy and pray. To pray you have to be attentive to God, not to the clamouring demands of others or the demands of your ego. For this to happen there has to be a time of withdrawal. This may be five minutes each day or an hour a week or even, possibly, a day a month. Some guru was once asked how longed he prayed for each day. He answered, 'I pray for an hour a day unless I'm very busy and then I pray for two hours.' It is precisely when we are very busy that it is necessary to stop and reflect.

John Wesley's wife, Susannah, had a very large family and she used to cover her head with a towel when she wanted to pray. The family all realised this and learned to be very quiet. There was a time when I used to have a good long bath for some peace and quiet. This was long before I started running and it was often on a Saturday night so that, hopefully, I could derive some inspiration for my sermon the following morning. The important requirement for any time of prayer is to find a time and space in the house when you give yourself the greatest chance of some peace and quiet. This might be first thing in the morning or last thing at night. My opportunities are greater since the family have grown up and flown the nest.

Having found space and time, then don't do anything! Just be. Don't strive to do anything. This is very much harder than it sounds. There is no need for any words. Words themselves can often provide a barrier between God and us in the same way that a very wordy liturgy can succeed in keeping God out. There is no room to let God in and there is certainly no opportunity to listen in most church services.

Prayer without words is not new! In the Old Testament there is the text, *'in quietness and trust shall be your strength.'* (Is. 30:15)

There is also the well-known verse in Psalm 46. Amidst all the noise and tumult of war and associated calamities the psalmist closes with the verse *'be still, and know that I am God.'* (Psalm, 46:10)

The Jerusalem bible has, *'pause a while and know that I am God.'* The old Latin version has, *'empty yourself and know that I am God.'*

This notion of emptying ourselves is much more helpful because there is no room for God until we are empty. A person once went to a guru for advice about how to find God. The guru poured out a cup of coffee and kept pouring even when the cup was full. This is an acted out example of the truism that there is no room for anything, let alone God, when we are full. The person who was seeking advice was too busy and too full of himself to take heed of what the guru had to say.

There are some more relevant texts.

It is good that one should wait quietly for the salvation of the Lord. (Lamentations, 3:26)

For God alone my soul waits in silence. (Ps. 62:1)

In I Kings 19 we find how God speaks to the prophet Elijah in a most unexpected way. Not in an earthquake, wind or fire but *'in the still small voice.'*

In the New Testament we read how Jesus often spent time alone with his Father.

He would withdraw to deserted places and pray. (Luke, 5:16)

In the last chapter we noted the well-known story of Martha and Mary. Martha is the one busy in the kitchen whilst Mary sits at the feet of Jesus. Jesus says that;

Mary has chosen the better part, which will not be taken away from her. (Luke, 10:42)

Paul writes:

The Spirit helps us in our weakness; for we do not know how to pray as we ought, but that very Spirit intercedes with sighs too deep for words. (Roms. 8:26)

Of course, all this is easier said than done! Rather like running a marathon, which is easier said than done! One of the problems is that it feels as though we are doing nothing and therefore we must be wasting our time. Not only that, if we are doing nothing, then things are outside our control. That is even more serious. Doing nothing means letting go and letting others get on with it. Withdrawing from the situation, even for a few moments, let alone minutes, might prove disastrous. How will they get on without me? More to the point, how will I get on if I'm no longer involved? Will I survive? Perhaps I'm overstating the case a little, but there is no doubt that these are very genuine fears amongst some people.

One of the secrets of long distance running is to stay in the present moment. If you start thinking about the number of miles you still have to run, it can be very dispiriting. Sometimes you can see runners in the distance, or even on the way back, and you think, 'I've got to run all that way, I'm never going to make it.' All of a sudden the run can become very daunting and there is a great temptation to give up and head for home. Similar things happen in the spiritual life. The future, for a whole host of reasons, can seem very fearful. How will I ever get through the next few hours, days or weeks? On the other hand, we can also be obsessed with what has happened. Both these tendencies take us away from the present moment and that is precisely where you can find your God; in the present moment.

Jesus, in a well-known passage about the birds of the air and the lilies of the field, finishes by saying:

So don't worry about tomorrow for tomorrow will bring worries of its own. Today's trouble is enough for today. (Matt. 6:34)

A more prosaic but up to date example is when a sports person has made a terrible shot or had a terrible game. The commentator says something like, 'They will just have to forget that shot and play for the next one.' That is being in the moment. It is not having a short-term memory. To put this in biblical terms, *'though your sins are like scarlet, they shall be like snow.'* (Isaiah 1:18)

God, apparently, has no memory.

There is a best-seller entitled '*The power of the Now*', [8] which has as its main thesis that silence and space all around us is one of the keys to entering inner peace. In the Now, the present moment, problems do not exist. In the Now, we discover that we are already complete and perfect. 'Now is the most precious things there is. Why is it the most precious thing? Firstly, because it is the *only* thing. It is all there is... Life is now. There was never a time when your life was *not* now. Secondly, the Now is the only point that can take you beyond the limited confines of the mind.

It is your only point of access into the timeless and formless realm of Being.'[9]

People use different methods for trying to overcome the distractions and stay in the present moment. One technique is simply to concentrate on your breathing. Another method is to repeat constantly a word or phrase. This gives the brain something to do. When you find your thoughts beginning to wander, you return to your breathing or your 'word'. As with running, it takes time and practice if any improvement is to take place. Physical posture also helps. Slouched in a chair tends to induce sleep. This is not the place to go into this in details. Books have been written which more than adequately explain these methods.[10]

Another way of looking at being in the present moment is to be more aware of what is happening around you. Some people call this mindfulness or attentiveness. Personally, I am not very good at this. Lucy is much better than I am and I continue to learn from her. My problem (one of them) is that I am always looking to move on to the next thing. My work as a minister and counsellor seemed to mean that I was always looking at my wristwatch. Turning up late for a service, a funeral, a meeting was not something I ever wanted to do. When training to be a marriage counsellor, it was drummed in to me that if you turned up late to meet a client, it gave completely the wrong message. The implication was that you had something important to do and, therefore, the assumption was that the client was less important. Since retirement I have become less neurotic about time and learned to 'turn aside' a lot more just to see.

'The practice of paying attention is as simple as looking twice at people and things you might just as easily ignore. To see takes time, like having a friend takes time. It is as simple as turning off the television to learn the song of a single bird. Why should anyone do such things? I cannot imagine, unless one is weary of crossing days off the calendar with no sense of what makes the last day different from the next. Unless one is weary of acting in what feels more like a television commercial than a life. The practice of paying attention offers no quick fix for such weariness, with guaranteed results printed on the side. Instead, it is one way into a different way of life full of treasure for those who are willing to pay attention to exactly where they are.'[11]

Exercise:

I will spend some time just being. I won't strive to do anything. When distractions come, as they will, I will concentrate on my breathing and/or constantly repeat a word or phrase.

To Ponder:

The Japanese warrior was captured by his enemies and thrown into prison. At night he could not sleep for he was convinced that he would be tortured in the morning.

Then the words of his master came to mind. "Tomorrow is not real. The only reality is now."

So he came to the present – and fell asleep.

The person over whom the future has lost its grip. How like the birds of the air and the lilies of the field. No anxieties for tomorrow. Total presence in the now. Holiness![12]

Chapter 5

Spectators

Palm Sunday. It just so happens that the London Marathon in 2014 took place on Palm Sunday. That is the day when the Christian Church has traditionally celebrated the entry of Jesus into Jerusalem. We are told that he rode on a donkey; the crowd laid branches on the road and shouted:

Hosanna to the Son of David! Blessed is the one who comes in the name of the Lord!
Hosanna in the highest heaven! (Matt. 21:9)

I wasn't riding on a donkey and the crowds weren't waving palm branches but they were certainly incredibly supportive and encouraging. My name was printed on the front of my T- shirt and so people often used to shout out my name. On one occasion, we were running along and things were unusually quiet when suddenly a loud voice boomed out, 'Come on, Malcolm, and get those legs moving.' Later on I just felt I needed to walk for a little while and when somebody shouted out, 'Keeping running, Malcolm,' I thought I had better make the effort and start running again.

The result was that the crowd started shouting, 'Malcolm, Malcolm, Malcolm.' As you can see, the crowd were immensely encouraging: 'Keep going, Malcolm, you are doing really well.' 'You are doing great, Malcolm, only another fifteen miles to go.' The comment I liked best was 'Keep it up, Malcolm, you can still win this.' What a wonderful comment. It goes without saying that I couldn't possibly win, but hearing that comment kept me going for quite a while. There were many children along the way who held out their hands wanting to do a high five. Some were counting how many they had achieved. Other people, especially towards the end, were handing out jelly babies because these are a good source of sugar and thereby promote some energy. I actually started with a good supply but these ran out towards the end and so I was glad of these wonderful spectators. Please note that I didn't know any of these people, they were all strangers, but they were being extremely kind and supportive by their words and actions. Some words in Paul's letter to the Thessalonians sprang to mind.

And we urge you, beloved, to admonish the idlers, encourage the faint-hearted, help the weak, be patient with all of them. See that none of you repays evil for evil, but always seek to do good to one another and to all. (1 Thess. 5:14–15)

Herein is that all important principle of encouraging people and being kind to one another, even if, and especially if, you don't know them. Encourage the faint-hearted. That was certainly me and I needed all the encouragement I could get. I once knew somebody in one of my congregations who took the trouble to find out if anyone from the congregation was in hospital. This lady, Rachel, was well into her eighties and could no longer attend church. However, she took it upon herself to write a card or letter to those who were in hospital even though she did not know them personally.

It can make all the difference to your day, especially if you are having a difficult time, if someone gives you some encouragement. Someone might simply smile at you, or ask how you are and genuinely want to know. There might be a phone call from someone you haven't heard from for ages and ages. On the other hand, you might have a conversation with your Big Issue seller and perhaps give them more than the cost of the magazine. Sometimes in our relationships things go horribly pear-shaped and you wonder about the right course of action. A useful maxim that was passed on to me is 'when in doubt, do the kindest thing.'

All the way round the course the spectators were really, really supportive and seemed to give me a lift when I needed it. I also received a lift from the many people I knew were praying for me. Many of them were actually in church worshipping. Many more had actually contributed to the charity I was running for, 'Help the Hospices'. I was committed to raising £2,000, but in the event I managed over £3,000. People were extremely kind and generous. I have to say that the donations, which kept coming in weeks before the big day, were a huge encouragement in my training. People had given so generously, I just had to keep on training. A group of supporters I have not yet mentioned were my close family, plus two friends.

Fifteen of the family were able to be present, including six grandchildren, and two who have yet to make an appearance into the big wide world. Their first gathering point was near to Canada Water tube station. It sounded a long way away, almost as if it were on another continent. Anyway, somehow we managed to see each other and it was great seeing some familiar faces to cheer me on my way. The next meeting point was near to Canary Wharf but, regrettably, it didn't happen. My supporters club were far too busy eating pizza. Since there were so many of them, the service was rather slow and so they missed me by 'just a few minutes'. I must have been running faster than they thought! These things happen. We hope to meet someone and then, often for very good reasons, they fail to turn up. Someone promises to do something and then they forget to carry out their promise. We are left with, at the very least, a feeling of disappointment, of being let down. This happens to all of us at one time or other. It seems to be part of the human condition. There are those who would argue that God is the only person you can rely on. God has promised to be with us at all times. Jesus said:

I will ask the Father, and he will give you another Advocate, to be with you for ever. (John, 13:17)

This is in connection with the promise of the Holy Spirit. Then again at the end of Matthew's gospel Jesus says:

And remember, I am with you always, to the end of the age. (Matt. 28:20)

St Paul writes:

For I am convinced that neither death, not life, nor angels, nor rulers, nor things present, nor things to come, nor powers, nor height, nor depth, will be able to separate us from the love of God in Christ Jesus our Lord. (Romans, 8: 38, 39)

God promises not to be an absent God. The promise is that God is always present and we can never be separated from that presence. The problem is that it doesn't always feel like that! There are times when it really does seem as if God is absent. Jesus himself shouts out that well-known cry of dereliction from the cross, *'My God, my God, why have you forsaken me?'* (Mark, 15:34)

My guess is that we feel God is absent when there is a lot going on in our lives. This could be the general busyness of family life, employment issues, and a strain in a relationship, financial worries, a serious illness, a bereavement, or any other of the many things that can afflict us in our everyday life. As we saw in chapter three, there can also be many things going on inside our heads. It feels sometimes as though we are in a crowded room and everybody is trying to talk to us at the same time. So much is going on there isn't the least possibility that we can focus on anything, let alone God.

Happily, my supporters club all turned up in force at Westminster. Was I glad to see them?

A big hug from Lucy was a lifesaver. I could have stayed longer but there was just a little further to go and so I pulled myself away and carried on. Knowing that people are watching you, and you may even be on a television camera, is a great incentive. I wonder whether our lives would be any different if we took on board the fact that God is watching us. For some people that very thought may seem very threatening because they have grown up with the impression that God is always looking out for an opportunity to wield a big stick. Not so. God is infinitely more loving than the most loving parent. A loving God is not waiting with a big stick in his hand so that he can inflict punishment upon us. Quite the reverse. Just as a loving parent doesn't wish any harm to come to their children, so God doesn't want any harm to come to us.

Is there anyone among you, if your child asks for bread will give a stone? Or if the child asks for a fish, will give a snake? If you then, who are evil, know how to give good gifts to your children, how much more will your Father in heaven give good things to those who ask him! (Matt. 7: 10–11)

God only desires what is best for us. God does not wish us any harm, pain or suffering. Let's be honest, a lot of our pain is self-inflicted, but that brings me back to running!

I was often encouraged by various comments when out training. I used to meet somebody taking his dog for a walk who always greeted me in the following manner, 'Good morning, my good sir, nice to see you. Hope you are well. You take care now.' I always found those words very encouraging. Perhaps it was the 'sir' that appealed to my vanity! I've not been called that since my days as a teacher. On the other hand, perhaps it was because this man is in a wheelchair. His name is Victor. One of these fine days I'll stop and have a longer chat with him when I've got enough puff back. The received wisdom for runners is that you are supposed to have enough breath to say 'good morning' but not enough for a conversation. I usually just about had enough for a short 'morning'.

On another occasion there was a man coming in the other direction to me but the path was quite narrow and only room for one to pass and so I stopped and waited for him. As he strolled past he said, 'I walked quite slowly because it looked as though you needed a break.' How very true and how very considerate of him. Some weeks later, another man stepped to one side as I jogged by, 'I didn't want to break your stride,' he said. This man seemed to sense that I was on a roll and really didn't want to stop. Both people were somehow tuned in to what I required at that particular time.

Then again, there was a local youth who rode up to me on his bicycle. He was clad in leather and various pieces of metal adorned his face. My immediate reaction was to fear that I was about to face a torrent of abuse or, at the very least, some jokey comments about my pathetic efforts. Nothing could have been further from the truth. 'Come on, mate,' he said, 'you can do it, right to the end.' How's that for encouragement? And how's that for revealing my prejudices about a young person?

Once I was passing two teenage girls on their way home from school. They shouted after me, 'Get those legs up, Granddad!' I thought it was quite funny at the time. At the other end of the age spectrum as I passed an older lady I said, 'I'm exhausted.' It happens that I was running uphill at the time – actually a very gentle gradient. Anyway, the lady replied as quickly as a flash, 'So am I, and I'm only walking.' Such comments, and they are all genuine, kept me going. That last one brought to mind the obvious thought that we are all at different stages on the spiritual journey. It is all too easy to assume that we all perceive God in exactly the same way, or that we all pray in the same way, or that we all worship in the same way and so on. In many ways we are all the same but in many ways we are all different. God must love variety! One day it was very, very windy and I was really struggling to run against the wind. A young man ran past me. He seemed to float along as though he didn't feel the wind. As he passed he said, 'It's not easy running this way is it?' My reply was, 'It's not easy running any way at my age,' but I doubt if he heard a word because he was long gone into the distance. I actually tried to keep up with him but failed after a couple of paces. My thoughts brought to mind that old adage 'pray as you can, not as you can't' which has often been translated as 'play as you can, not as you can't'. In other words, it is you in all your uniqueness that matters. You have to do those things that accord with your capabilities.

45

Of course, we are usually capable of much more than we actually achieve, but that is another story. So it was that all these people supported me in one way or another and so it was that training almost became enjoyable and so it was that I crossed the finishing line of the marathon. Let me fill you in with more of the details of that memorable day.

Exercise:

I wonder whom I could possibly encourage today. What action do I need to take?
How many times in the last 24 hours have I actually been discouraging.

To Ponder:

If God were looking at my life right now what would he/she see?

Chapter 6

The Big Day

Nervous? I wasn't exactly nervous in the sense of having butterflies and, to my surprise, I didn't have a delicate bowel but I was very, very apprehensive. The big day had finally arrived after all the years of preparation. Could I actually achieve what I had set out to do or was it a bridge too far? Would I trip up and sprain my ankle? Would I really last the course or would I drop out? What would the weather be like – too hot, too cold or windy? Would I embarrass myself in front of the crowd, let alone the television cameras, and need an urgent loo break? Was I really about to run in the London Marathon? Would I be able to get there in time?

I had cut my toenails to reduce any chance of too much friction and had my hair cut to make me more streamlined. I would do anything to give me even the smallest edge. I discovered though, that it was quite unnecessary to remove my beard. People who take part in the Tour de France have discovered that recent tests at a specialised aerodynamics department showed that facial hair made less than one second's difference over 40km. I reckoned, given my likely time, that my beard would make no difference at all.

As recommended by the experts, I was also very careful to eat plenty of pasta for a few days beforehand. They call this 'carbo-loading'. I was willing to do anything if it gave me a better chance. The experts also say that nothing you can do in the week before a big race will make any difference at all to your performance. It is too late to start doing anything new. In fact, the received wisdom is to not do very much running in the days immediately before. You actually have to considerably decrease your output. The theory is that on the big day you will be completely rested, relaxed and raring to go. That is the theory which I was about to put to the test.

I knew that I would need to get up at about 5am, so in order for this not to be too disruptive on the day, for a few days beforehand I went to bed earlier than usual so that I got up much earlier than usual - even before the dawn chorus! Breakfast was much bigger than usual. Plenty of water, a large bowl of oats, a banana, plus toast covered in honey. As I said, this was much bigger than usual, but note, there was no bacon. This is not the occasion for a full English breakfast. Fatty food is not recommended for fear of inducing heartburn. I also took a banana for on the way to Greenwich.

On signing up for the race, one is regularly sent blogs via email with interesting titles like '5 foods you need. Plus 10 exercises every runner should do', 'tiny workout tweaks, big results. Plus, boost your metabolism', '5 worst training mistakes. Plus, 8 problems only runners will understand.' These are only a sample of the blogs. I tell you if I had had the time to read them all, and put them into practice, I would have turned out to be a combination of Murray, Nadal, Federer and Djokovic. A cloned Superman. Me? You must be joking! I did, however, take notice of one blog entitled, '5 things not to do before a marathon.' Firstly, don't eat too close to a run because this might cause cramp and nausea. Secondly, don't perform a static warm up but a dynamic one. For example, lunges, arm swings, leg swings ankle bounces and gentle jogging, these will help to reduce muscle friction. Thirdly, don't eat salad or vegetables. Although these are very healthy foods, they contain fibre and therefore may cause difficulties on the way. Fourthly, don't drink orange juice. This is a sugary drink and may result in an energy dip or cause acid reflux. Fifthly, don't drink too close to a run otherwise you may need to take a loo break on the way. Other blogs contain different suggestions but the one I liked best was 'just turn up'.

There was also a blog entitled '5 signs to show you are marathon ready.' According to that one I was ready and raring to go.

Fortunately, my eldest son, Oliver, had recently moved to Leatherhead with his family so that was my first pit stop. Having arisen in good time, I arrived there about seven o'clock and then Olly was able to drive me to the nearest tube station. On race day, all runners are able to travel on the London Underground and S.E. railways free of charge. That's a very worthwhile bonus. I can't think of any more at the moment! There is a gradual build-up of passengers as the tube nears London Bridge and you can see by their apparel, and looks of excitement (apprehension?), who the runners are. On the train from London Bridge to Greenwich I was sitting with three lads whose combined age was probably less than mine. They were reminiscing about previous runs and elaborating on which part of their bodies hurt the most during a race. Was it their calves, their ankles or their hamstrings? I was totally bemused by their conversation but in the end I had to interrupt them by saying, 'When you get to my age, lads, everything hurts.'

The London marathon has three starting points but mine was in the traditional one of Greenwich Park. Before the day, you are sent, among other things, a red plastic sack in which you can place any items you are not going to run with, for example, your track suit. There are large lorries that take these sacks according to your race number. They have to be handed in before 9.30am. I arrived there at about 9am so there was time for a loo break and a quick phone call to Lucy. Having handed in one's over-clothes, you are left to hang around until the start. Fortunately, the weather was fine. Indeed, it was a lovely morning. Just right for a gentle stroll round Greenwich Park.

Eventually, people move over to their designated starting zone, which is based on one's projected finishing time. Naturally, I was near the back. There is nothing to do except stand around and maybe chat to the people next to you. As luck would have it, I found myself standing next to a man from Yorkshire. In the course of conversation, I discovered he was from Bradford and not only that, he was a season ticket holder for Bradford City Football Club. I say this because my wife's niece's husband used to play for City when they were in the top division. Our conversation finished with the guy saying, 'Next time you see Wayne Jacobs tell him he was a Bradford City legend!'

This was a totally unexpected encounter. How could I have ever imagined such a thing would happen? It seems to me that part of the secret of an interesting life is to remain open to possibilities. You could put a Christian slant on this by saying that God is a God of surprises.[13] There is often a temptation to close down possibilities by saying things like, 'that won't work' or 'I've seen it all before' or 'I can't be bothered' or 'this is boring' or simply going through life with a very low level of awareness. Possibilities simply do not arise because we are in our own little world. Moreover, there is a high risk of experiencing something without giving time to reflect on it. One can take a photograph to show the world on Facebook that you have visited Edinburgh Castle without really taking the care and time actually to 'see' the castle. Looking is easy, seeing is somewhat more difficult. I digress.

The start of the race was 10am. But since I was so far back, it took me 25 minutes, moving very slowly, to reach the starting line. In other words, there was about an hour when I was doing very little except standing still, moving very, very slowly, talking to those around me and waving at the distant television camera. Once over the line, the race began. I couldn't believe it. I was actually running in the London Marathon. My dreams had come true. This was a thought that kept me going for a little while as I listened to the background patter of hundreds of feet. People of all shapes and sizes were running. What a colourful spectacle it was.

Whilst running, apart from the obvious, there are two things that you can do to take your mind off things. You can be aware of things happening outside of yourself. On one occasion I remember passing a mortuary with its public entrance clearly visible. Was somebody trying to tell me something? Another example would be to look at the tea clipper, the Cutty Sark, and wonder about all the voyages it went on or muse about where it got its name from.

Apparently, the name is derived from the poem 'Tam O'Shanter' by Robert Burns. The poem is about a farmer called Tam who is chased by the scantily-clad witch named 'Nannie', dressed only in a 'cutty sark' – an archaic Scottish name for a short nightdress. The character of Nannie in the poem is depicted as the figurehead that adorns Cutty Sark's bow. Now you know! You can also be aware of the all the different runners around you, in all their many guises.

I found myself running behind someone dressed as a telephone box with the word 'Samaritans' printed on. That's handy, I thought, if I get into difficulties I can ring them up. Then I followed some young ladies who looked very attractive. It seemed to take ages before we reached that well-known landmark, the Cutty Sark in Greenwich. Surely I couldn't be getting tired already. There was a long way to go. On another occasion I ran past a brass band that was walking along. The trombonist very nearly knocked me over with his slide! Then I actually passed a team of Kenyan runners. I couldn't believe it. Maybe they were having an off day or not really running at all but going on a sightseeing tour. There were people dressed up as rhinos, a karaoke singer, a bride dressed in a complete wedding outfit and many, many other different attires – some serious and some not so serious.

The second thing you can do, as well as being aware of the sights and sounds around you, is to be aware of what is happening within you. In other words, you become very aware of your own body, your breathing pattern, your hydration, your aches and pains and your general well-being – or lack of it! Thankfully, there are lots of water stations along the route and even some places where energy drinks can be obtained, and so hydration should not be a problem. I confess that when I'm out training on my own, this is the mode I am most often in. Yes, there is the Brittany Ferry just leaving Portsmouth Harbour, there is an Egret on the water's edge, there is the wonderful smell of a fish and chip shop wafting over the airwaves, there is one of my neighbours cutting their grass. I must remember to keep my mouth shut there are a lot of flies about. Is that someone from church coming in my direction? I hope they don't recognise me otherwise I might have to stop and talk to them. What shall I have for lunch today? Is it my turn to cook dinner later on? What shall we have today? Is the tide in or out today? Will I be able to get all the way round on the path or will I have to make a detour because of high tide? As you can see, in the main, I was in my own bubble.

In this mode, which you could almost call meditation, I often became aware of thoughts that were new to me. Most of the ideas in this book have arisen as I have been out running. It is as though there is an inner voice that is speaking. The strange thing is that it doesn't feel as though I am talking to myself. I know what I sound like and it's usually pretty boring. Would it be too fanciful to call this voice God? This is the reason I don't listen to music when running. Some do and find it very beneficial and it helps to relieve the boredom on a long run but I prefer to remain in my bubble with a minimum of distractions so that I am open to that voice within.

Running round London there was so much happening in the immediate environment that it was virtually impossible to get into this second mode of being. There will be more of this in the next chapter. Somehow, I remember getting to Tower Bridge – but that's not even half way. I discovered later that I actually appeared on television whilst crossing the bridge. It was very briefly you understand. If you blinked you would have missed me but there I was, two seconds of fame.

Once over the bridge, there is a section where you can see all the front runners coming back on the other side of the dual carriage way. My thought was that I would soon be joining them. How mistaken I was. We had to trek all-round the Isle of Dogs. It seemed to be never-ending. All I wanted to do was reach the Thames embankment then I could see Big Ben and know that maybe, just maybe, I could actually finish. I had to tell myself that it didn't matter what the other runners were up to or how far in front they were. The only important thing was whether I was going to finish or not.

I confess, there were times when I just had to take a little break and do some walking. I needed to catch my second wind. I was 'feeling the burn'. This is a physiological condition but far too complicated for me to go into here. All I know is I was beginning to hurt and doubts were starting to set in. Somehow, by putting one foot in front of the other, the Thames came into view. Passing Waterloo Bridge I remember getting emotional because for the very first time I thought that was a good chance I was going to make it, although my feet were getting really sore. I was used to running mainly on soft surfaces but this had been on hard, unforgiving concrete. Soon the embankment station came into view, then Big Ben, Westminster, Birdcage Walk, Buckingham Palace and, finally, the Mall. I had done it.

Because of the large numbers involved, there is no possibility of your loved ones being at the finishing line to greet you and so I gave a big hug to the young lady who handed me my finisher's medal! You collect your bag of goodies, water and energy drink, T-shirt and some nibbles and collect the bag that was handed in at the start, and then you walk, very slowly in my case, to the meet and greet area in Horse Guards parade. It was absolutely wonderful to see Lucy and Oliver there. Now I had two bodies to lean on. We walked to the Queen Elizabeth Centre where 'Help the Hospices' had organised a reception. They laid on an energy drink and a bowl of pasta. More importantly, they also laid on some massage. Oh, what bliss. My legs were gently massaged into life.

When I felt that sufficient life had returned, we walked to Oliver's car, which was about 15 minutes away. This time I had the services of my granddaughter Georgia, as well as Lucy, to lean on! After a short stop at Leatherhead to change cars we eventually arrived home only to discover that I could hardly get out of the car! I had simply stiffened up almost to the point of becoming rigid. Some heavy lifting gear was required and there was none to hand. Eventually, and with a great effort, I managed to prise myself up and out of my seat. Climbing the stairs presented even more of a challenge. It was as though I had an elephant in each pocket. Perhaps these elephants were related to the ones I met after my very first cross-country run. What wonders a hot bath can do. Of course, the experts reckon that a cold ice bath is much more beneficial for your muscles but I'll leave that to them. Anyway, we didn't have enough ice. A hot bath was what I needed and so that's what I had. Surprisingly, the adrenalin was still flowing quite freely and as I lay there soaking up the delicious warmth, I managed to complete The Observer crossword. As you might have guessed, it was a rather long bath! The one thing that made me finish bathing was not just that the water was getting cold but the smell of food wafting up from the kitchen. By this time I realised I was getting hungry. Never did a full English taste so wonderful. I was no longer worried about training and what to eat and what not to eat. I had done it. I could eat what I wanted! Thus ended a very, very long, exhausting, but exhilarating day.

Exercise:

When did I last have a 'big' day? What made it so special?

To Ponder:

Some people actually said they were in awe of me completing this feat. Let me tell you what awe is. On September 5, 1977, the spacecraft Voyager 1 was launched from NASA. The aim was to study the planets Saturn, Jupiter, Neptune and Uranus and then proceed to the outer solar system. It was a major scientific achievement to solve the mathematically complex puzzle of plotting the trajectory. For this to happen, of course, the universe has to move in very predictable ways. The craft is moving at a speed of 38,120 mph and is travelling 325 million miles per year. As of September 2012, sunlight took 16.89 hours to reach Voyager 1.

It is expected to reach the Oort cloud in about 300 years and take about 30,000 years to pass through it. Planet earth is seen as a 'pale blue dot' – a tiny, tiny fraction of a pixel. Now *that* is awe-inspiring.

Chapter 7

P.B.

Personal Best. You may have noticed that I have not yet disclosed my time. Well, here it is. Six hours, twenty-three minutes and thirty-six seconds! Amazingly, I was actually in the same race as Mo Farah, the double Olympic and World champion. The reality is though that he crossed the starting line about half an hour before me and so he had a really good start over me. If we had started together, who knows what the outcome would have been! Of course I could have gone quicker if only the weather had not been so hot, if only I had been a bit fitter, if only I had relaxed a bit more and just enjoyed the day, if only... Sometimes we can go through life saying just that, if only. My dear mother used to enjoy a game of cards. You always knew when she had been dealt a bad hand because she scrunched up her face. When her hand was good there was no reaction. Life is about playing the cards we have been dealt to the very best of our ability. We can't play the cards we haven't be dealt. If only...

The important thing for me was not the time, or the finisher's medal, or the T-shirt, although it was good to have them. The main point was that I had finished in a personal best time. Since it was my very first marathon, and my last, that goes without saying. I was not trying to be like Mo Farah (as if!).

There are times in our lives when we wish we could be like somebody else. How I wish I could play the piano like Lang Lang or Oscar Peterson, or play football like David Beckham, or look like George Clooney, or be as funny as Paul Merton, or be able to write a good story like J.K. Rowling or, or, or, – the list is endless. God only requires me to be me and to do my personal best. There is already a Lang Lang, an Oscar, a David, a George, a Paul and a J.K. – why would he want another one? On the other hand, there is only one of me – and one is quite enough for anybody.

Whilst out training, I remember somebody shouting across to me, 'Are you training for the Olympics?' They were joking of course! That is the good news about the Christian life. We are not training for a competition. What other people do is up to them. The only thing that matters is how I lead my life. Interestingly, as we saw in chapter one, St Paul has the following passage about running the race.

Do you not know that in a race the runners all compete, but only one receives the prize? Run in such a way that you may win it. Athletes exercise self-control in all things; they do it to receive a perishable garland, but we an imperishable one. (1 Cor. 9: 24–25)

This passage is not about competition. After all, only one person wins the prize, which in those days would have been a pine wreath or some such. The point that Paul is making in this metaphor is that in a contest all compete and everyone tries as hard as they can. Everyone takes it seriously, otherwise there is no point in entering. Today we might say that 'this life is not a dress rehearsal'. There is only one 'race' and thereby it is of the utmost importance that we give of our best. Of course, if you are to stand any chance at all, some training is necessary. Athletes must be disciplined and exercise self-control over all aspects of their life.

Personally, I find trying to be a Christian extremely difficult. The heart of the gospel can be found in the collection of verses that have been called the Sermon on the Mount (Matt. chapters 5, 6 and 7). There are verses in there about forgiveness, loving your enemies, turning the other cheek, going the second mile, giving to charity, fasting, and praying. Whoever imagined for one moment that being a Christian was easy? Yes, the bible can speak comforting words at times but there are also many words that make me feel very uncomfortable.

What about not storing up treasures on earth *'where moth and rust consume and where thieves break in and steal?'* (Matt. 6:19)

How do we respond to that in our consumer-led society where some people's motto is 'I shop therefore I am'? I am very much part of that society so do I need to spend money on books that then spend their days gathering dust on my shelves? Do I really need something or do I just want it? Millions of people in the world still do not have access to clean water let alone any kind of luxury goods, which we, in the West, simply take for granted.

My generation took for granted free education, free health and dental care and still takes for granted the right to travel anywhere in the world whenever we want to, usually by flying. It is a well-known fact that climate change is here to stay and is getting worse. Scientists have now agreed on this. It is also a fact that flying produces carbon, which is a major contributor to climate change. Does this matter or do I just go on doing what I want when I want regardless of anybody else – especially those living near the sea whose lives will be upturned when sea levels start to rise. The

Christian response must be something to do with this one world, this fragile planet that we believe God has created and who has given us the responsibility to look after it. If nothing else, do we have a responsibility towards our children and grandchildren and their progeny?

If we are really to give our personal best then maybe, just maybe, these are some of the matters that we have to seriously reflect on. No doubt those who know their Sermon on the Mount will recall the verse, *'Be perfect, therefore, as your heavenly Father is perfect.'* (Matt. 5:48)

This suggests that doing one's best is not good enough, only perfection will fit the bill. Please note that being perfect is not the same as perfectionism. There is something obsessive about perfectionists. Indeed, they can be so obsessive that they would prefer to do things themselves rather than ask anybody else. They think that they are the only person who will do the job to the required standard. One could argue that these people also want to control everything. If anybody else is allowed in, who knows what will happen? Maybe things will start to go wrong and chaos will ensue. This is not what the text means by being perfect. Indeed, some argue that it is precisely when we are imperfect, when we are making mistakes, then we have the possibility of growing in the spiritual life. If we are perfect then there is nowhere else to go! *'We grow spiritually much more by doing it wrong than by doing it right.'*[14] Mark Townsend has written a book called *The Gospel of Falling Down* with the subtitle *The beauty of failure, in an age of success.*[15] If perfection means anything, it means somehow incorporating all our failures, our weakness, our imperfections into our spirituality. In a word, perfection is about recognising that we are human after all! As Paul puts it in his letter to the Romans, *'we have all sinned and fallen short of the glory of God.'* (Roms. 3:23)

He also writes those enigmatic words, *'When I am weak, then I am strong.'* (2 Cor. 12:10) Biblical commentators have given a deal of thought as to what the word 'perfection' means in the original text. Christians are certainly supposed to imitate God, but to be as perfect as God is surely an impossibility. That would make us God! Maybe Jesus is simply setting a goal for us to aim at although the attainment of it is impossible. An alternative view is gained if we look at the context of the verse. The immediately preceding verses talk about loving your enemies and praying for those who persecute you (verse 44); God providing sun and rain on the good/righteous and on the evil/unrighteous alike (verse 45); and about loving not only those who love you – even tax collectors and gentiles do that. Similarly, don't just greet your brothers and sisters *'even Gentiles do the same'* (verse 46 and 47). In other words, being a Christian is not common sense! It is very often doing the opposite. Especially, Christianity is about including people whom society has excluded. The Kingdom of God is a community of people where no one is excluded. The only people who are excluded are those who do so by their own choice.

In a word, Jesus is here talking about love, a love that reaches even to a believer's enemies and persecutors. This is easier said than done but this is perfection. Paul says something similar when writing to the Christians at Colossae:

Above all, clothe yourselves with love, which binds everything together in perfect harmony. (Col. 3:14)

The root meaning of the word 'perfect' is undivided, whole, and complete. Hence, when the verse asks people to be perfect, it means in the same way that God treats people, that is, in a way that is undivided or whole. God's love is complete, without defect or blemish. There is a parallel sentiment in the Old Testament where the holiness of God is intended to bring about holiness in the community.

Speak to all the congregation of the people of Israel and say to them: You shall be holy, for me the Lord your God am holy. (Lev. 19:2)

'If there is such a thing as human perfection, it seems to emerge precisely from how we handle the imperfection that is everywhere, especially our own. What a clever place for God to hide holiness, so that only the humble and earnest will find it!'[16]

The one thing all are agreed on is that humans continue to do wrong and that perfection is something to strive for. Happily, the grace of God, the undeserved forgiveness of God, comes to our rescue and allows us to move forward. Our personal best is something to strive for. It is certainly not perfection but in any moment of time the hope is that it is our best.

Exercise:

In what ways have I achieved a 'personal best'?

Is there something that needs to shift in me so that I can follow the example of Jesus through his life and the Sermon on the Mount?

Who do I need to learn to love?

Where do I need God's grace in my life right now?

To Ponder:

One day the disciples wanted to know what sort of person was best suited to discipleship.

Said the Master, 'The kind of person who, having only two shirts, sells one and with the money buys a flower.'[17]

Chapter 8

P.S.

Postscript. Believe it or not the day after the Big Day I actually managed to get out of bed without too much stiffness. Yes, I was still physically very tired but I was moving and still breathing. For that I was very thankful because some poor soul had actually died running the race. How tragic is that? My feet were quite tender and I did have a big black toe, but apart from that I was more or less back to normal, although certainly not ready for any kind of exercise. By Thursday I was beginning to feel it would be a good idea to go for a little jog just to make sure I could still operate. I stopped and started for about an hour and that was quite enough. Then time slipped by and we had two weeks holiday and guess what? I realised I was putting on weight again and beginning to feel very lazy. The time had come to put on my running shoes again and so six weeks after the marathon I went for a jog. It is absolutely amazing how fitness disappears if you don't keep at it. There is that well known aphorism 'use it or lose it'. In six weeks I had almost lost it completely. Running quite slowly for an hour was quite enough. How I managed to complete a marathon

I will never know. In truth, God alone knows. Miracles still happen.

Now I go out for an hour's jog about three times a week. What will happen when winter comes only time will tell. For the moment the weather is fine but even so the experience is quite different. Now there is nothing to aim for and so my motivation is somewhat weaker. All I can do is try to run a little faster each time. That is easier said than done because I am not a fast runner. Indeed some people walk faster than I run. The point is that I try to improve my P.B. even if it is only the odd second here and there. My stopwatch has become very important. I need to measure my progress against something. As a matter of interest, over the last few weeks I have improved my time by eight minutes. That might not seem a lot but to me it is a mountain. All we are asked to do in life is to *'run with perseverance the race that is set before us.'* (Hebs. 12: 1)

Would you believe it? Whilst on one of these little runs I actually fell and banged by big toe: the black one and the very toe where the maggots had been. To cut a long story short my toe fell off – not my toe just the nail.

One thing is for sure, I have no intention of running another marathon. I've been there, done that and got the T-shirt. It's all very well trying to keep one's body in shape but there are limits to what you can ask the body to do. At least, that's what my body is telling me 'enough is enough'. You've done the Great South Run, the Portsmouth Half and the London Marathon, now you can give me a rest and take it a bit easier. Just let those hip joints and knee joints lead a more sedentary life.

I'm not at all sure what God has in store for me now. One thing is certain there will be surprises along the way. The great surprise for me, which I still can't get over, is that I actually managed to complete the London marathon.   It can only be because God was with me all the way, through thick and thin - as she always is!

Exercise:

I wonder if I could try a little bit of physical exercise. Nothing too strenuous to start with.

To Ponder:

In my 'race' through life, do I measure myself up to anything or anybody? What is my yardstick? Am I improving or not? How do I know?

Chapter 9

P.F.S.

I wonder if some of you have read this book very quickly because you wanted to know if I had actually completed the course and if there were any side effects. In rushing through, you probably overlooked the exercises at the end of each chapter. Your challenge now is to go back and spend time on those exercises.

Exercise:

Which of the exercises did I rush through or not bother with? I wonder why I missed them out. Can I find the time to go through them all more slowly over the next few weeks?

To Ponder:

When things get difficult in your life, how do you react? Do you quickly rush on to the next thing? Bury your head in the sand and hope it will go away? Laugh it off? Or work at it and see what emerges?

References

1. Rothwell, Malcolm, *Journeying with God*, Epworth press, 2001

2. Taylor, Barbara Brown, *An Altar in the World*, Canterbury press, 2013 ibid. p. 37–38

3. Radcliffe, Paula, *How to Run*, Simon and Schuster, 2011

4. McChesney, Richard, *You know you are a runner*, Strictly Business Limited, 2013. p.14

5. Allan, Nicholas, *Jesus' Day Off*, Red Fox, 2002

6. Yaconelli, Mike, *Messy Spirituality*, Hodder & Stoughton, 2001. p110–111 Tolle, Eckhart, *The Power of the Now*, Hodder & Stoughton, 1999

7. ibid. p.43

8. There is a plethora of books about silence and meditation. The following are very accessible;

9. O'Rourke, Benignus, *Finding Your Hidden Treasure*, DLT, 2010

10. Small, Simon, *From the Bottom of the Pond*, O Books, 2008

11. Laird, Martin, *Into the Silent Land*, DLT, 2006 Taylor, op.cit.p.33

12. De Mello, Anthony, *The Song of the Bird*, Image books, 1984. p.21

13. Hughes, Gerald W. God of Surprises, DLT, 1985
14. Rohr, Richard, Falling Upward, a Spirituality for the Two Halves of Life, Jossey- Bass, 2011 p.xxii
15. Townsend, Mark, The Gospel of Falling Down, O Books, 2007
16. Rohr, op. cit.
17. De Mello, Anthony, One Minute Wisdom, Anand-Press, 1985.

Note: All biblical references are taken from the New RSV.